Born to Coach

Josh Schertz and the Remarkable Rise of the LMU Railsplitters

By Paul Erland

With Scott Erland

Copyright © 2016 Paul Erland

All rights reserved.

ISBN:1517457866
ISBN-13:9781517457860

DEDICATION

To basketball coaches everywhere – and to all those who hold the game in their hearts.

TABLE OF CONTENTS

	Introduction: You Have to Be a Little…	Page 7
1	Into the Madness	Page 13
2	From Assists to Assistant	Page 20
3	Will an Itch Lead to a Niche?	Page 28
4	A Plateau Reached – Twenty Wins	Page 37
5	Practicing for Perfection	Page 48
6	Character, Not Characters	Page 57
7	"It's Just What He Does"	Page 66
8	Coaches: Thick as Thieves?	Page 75
9	Schemes and Themes	Page 83
10	"I Don't Get Paid to Coach"	Page 91
11	A Nice Way to Live Your Life	Page 99
12	Onward and Upward	Page 108

INTRODUCTION

YOU HAVE TO BE A LITTLE...

It's almost the first day of summer, but basketball is in the air at the B. Frank "Tex" Turner Arena—literally and figuratively. The Lincoln Memorial University team camp for area high schools and middle schools is in full swing. The camp is no drills and all competition, with each team guaranteed a minimum of seven games over four days, and the players promised "full exposure" to college coaches. On this particular afternoon there doesn't appear to be many, if any, of these exalted personages in attendance, but that doesn't deter the campers, who still have their parents and their own coaches to impress. So the play is spirited, even if few of the players have a college basketball career in their future, to be frank. (And it is altogether fitting and proper to do so, when you're inside the *B. Frank Turner Arena*.)

Basketball camp at Turner Arena

It's the day after the last game of the 2014-15 NBA season. The Golden State Warriors, a team I followed avidly all year, have just polished off the Cleveland Cavaliers and their megastar, the admirable LeBron James, to win the championship, four games to two. The series will be memorable for the Warriors' poise in response to LeBron's historic performance, and almost as much for the game-by-game strategies of the two rookie head coaches as for the actual games.

I watched just about every one of Golden State's games this year, thanks to the NBA League Pass and my DVR. It was an exhilarating ride, following a team whose devotion to egoless, root-for-each-other play not only culminated in a championship and the league's third-best record ever, but was a reaffirmation of how beautiful the game of basketball can be.

For a basketball junkie like me, the high of that ride will last at most for several more days, before withdrawal pains set in.

So I'm here in Harrogate, Tennessee to interview Josh Schertz, the coach of LMU's men's basketball team. In just seven seasons as the Railsplitters' head coach, Schertz is already the school's second all-time leader in wins. (Dean Bailey has 338, but it took him 27 years to amass them.) Schertz has led LMU to six straight 20-win seasons and five consecutive NCAA Tournament appearances. The Railsplitters' 73 consecutive weeks ranked in the Division II national poll (with three separate number one rankings) is the fourth-longest such run in the history of Division II men's basketball. What makes the resume particularly impressive is the fact that before Schertz's arrival, LMU was a desolate hinterland, so to speak, of the basketball world, with only 39 wins over the five previous seasons.

My interest in Schertz is twofold: There's the spectacular success, and then there's the fact that my son, Scott, played for him for two years. In 2008, Schertz's first year at LMU, Scott, who was there on a baseball scholarship, was a walk-on for the basketball team.

That year's team was 14-14, including 8-8 in conference play (a startling improvement over the previous year's 1-13 effort). The next season, the Railsplitters reached 20 wins for the first time ever in their NCAA history. I didn't get to see many games, but from what I did see I was impressed by the team's intelligence and defensive effort. (As a player, I was smart enough, but I never could play defense. I tell Schertz I couldn't have played for him, and he says, "I couldn't have played for me, either.") And I was taken by the sight of this Schertz, a small Jewish fellow in a neatly pressed suit, surrounded by giants, talking softly, coolly and composedly.

Coach Schertz with some of his hardware

Whenever Scott talked about Schertz, he described how obsessive he was about basketball, how demanding he was, but how fair he was, and how honest. After he graduated, Scott went to work in LMU's athletic department, and there he got to know Schertz a lot better. Who he got to know, it sounded like to me, was a man endowed (or burdened) with all the characteristics above, only more so.

I wanted to know about the obsession.

I fell in love with basketball more than fifty years ago, as a pathologically shy adolescent. When everyone else was hanging out or doing normal teenage things, I was shooting hoops, often by myself. As a senior in high school, I skipped the prom, and went to the park to play ball. (A couple of wags on the prom committee put up a sign on the door of the gymnasium, reading "We'd like to thank Paul Erland for the use of the gym.") I played basketball in college, ending up as my school's all-time leading scorer (I'm still in third place), and then in Europe for a couple of years. My playing career ended right around the time Josh Schertz was born, in 1975. That doesn't mean I quit playing—I didn't, there was just no *career* involved.

Somewhere around my mid-twenties, my exasperated mom told me one day, "You sure have wasted a lot of time in your life playing basketball." I was thunderstruck, but I realized in due time—that is, twenty-five years or so later—that she was right. I gave up the game for good when I was fifty. Reluctantly.

I'm 65 now, a generation older than Josh Schertz. At the end of last season, Schertz signed a lifetime contract with LMU, insuring that he'll be able to coach the game he loves until he's at least my age, and probably beyond that. (How many people retire from an obsession?)

Among the hundreds of players at the LMU summer camp, maybe a handful will hold on to basketball their livelong life.

How to explain it, this long infatuation with…a *game*?

Well, to start with, as Josh Schertz puts it soon after we meet up:

"You have to be a little off."

CHAPTER 1

INTO THE MADNESS

Josh Schertz says he knew he wanted to be a coach after reading one book. The book was John Feinstein's *A March to Madness*, subtitled *The View from the Floor in the Atlantic Coach Conference*. Feinstein, whose most famous book, *A Season on the Brink*, written in 1986, was Everything You Always Wanted to Know but Were Afraid to Ask about the prickly Bobby Knight and his Indiana University basketball team, wrote *A March to Madness* in 1998. Chronicling a season (1996-97) of competition in the ACC, its leading characters were coaches Dean Smith of North Carolina and Mike Krzyzewski of Duke.

"I read it from cover to cover," Schertz recalls. "I thought, *how cool is this?*"

Schertz was twenty-two, and he'd had a coaching feeler already, even though he had another year of eligibility as a player.

"My dad had a friend at Florida Atlantic," he recalls. "They had a G. A. (graduate assistant) position open. They'd brought me down to interview in April."

It was the summer after his junior season at Piedmont University in Winston-Salem, North Carolina. "The only place that let me play," he says. It was a pretty good gamble, as Schertz had led the country in assists. Even so, he saw that he might have to make a choice, between playing and coaching the next year. But by July he hadn't heard anything, so he assumed he wasn't going to get the job.

"I wanted to play more anyway," he says, "but I knew it was a good opportunity." It would also allow him to be near his family. A couple of years earlier, while playing ball at an NAIA school in Florida, he'd met a girl and had a child. The girl was in school, so he got married, quit basketball for a year and worked two jobs. Then he got into Webber University (Babson Park, Florida), where he played for a year before moving on to Piedmont.

Up until then, he'd had no inkling that he'd ever be a coach. "I was going to either teach elementary school or work with special-needs kids," he says. Toward one of those ends, he was pursuing an Education degree with an emphasis in Physical Education.

Schertz as a player at Webber, looking for another assist

Feinstein's book turned the tide. He decided he did indeed want to be a coach. He talked to his own coach, and began to suspect that he might just be looking through rose-colored glasses.

"I thought you just started in the ACC," he laughs.

The coach gave him a more realistic view. He recommended that he play his remaining year, graduate with his Education degree, try to get on as a JV coach or a high-school assistant, and work his way up the ladder — like everyone else did.

"That was what I planned to do," he says. Then, late in July, he got the call from Florida

Atlantic, offering him the G. A. position. He had to make a quick decision: Move to south Florida and coach, or play his senior season.

"I had no clue," he says. "I didn't have any knowledge of the game, to speak of, let alone any idea about the coaching business."

He decided to take the job.

More than any other college coach, Schertz growing up admiring Dean Smith. (He never had to endure, as I did, Smith's infuriating four corners offense.) In 1997, the year Schertz embarked on his coaching career, Smith became the all-time winningest coach in college basketball. His North Carolina team went to the Final Four that year, losing in the semis to eventual champion Arizona.

Dean Smith

Like Schertz, Smith was pegged as coaching material while still a player. He was a reserve on the Kansas teams that won a national championship in 1952 and were runners-up the year after, and in his book Feinstein relates how Kansas's legendary coach, Phog Allen, had Smith, starting in his junior year, teach the offense and defense to football players joining the team late.

After graduation and a stint in the Air Force, Smith was hired as an assistant at North Carolina. Three years later, in 1961, he became the head coach. According to Feinstein, he went into it with modest expectations. "'I thought I'd try it,' he said, 'and if it didn't work out I could always go back and be a high school coach.'"

That eventuality almost came to pass. After one middling record and one good one, there came Smith's only losing season in the ACC, followed by a mediocre start the next season that led to Smith, famously, being hung in effigy.

Smith, of course, righted the ship and set sail on his illustrious career, but the story of his first few years is not uncommon, illustrating in a way what may be the first fact about the coaching profession: More fail than succeed.

Feinstein recounts Dean Smith's frequent assertion of how crucial Catherine Marshall's book *Beyond Our Selves,* and in particular a chapter called "The Power of Helplessness," was to his coaching career. His sister sent him the book after the effigy incident, and Smith said it helped him learn how to shut out external voices and focus on what was important.

Feinstein's book having given *him* a focus, Schertz headed homeward to Florida, determined to make good on his first coaching job, even though there would no monetary remuneration involved. That job consisted, for the most part, of "laundry and logistics." The team had no manager, and Schertz handled those tasks.

His days began before dawn and ended near midnight: He worked from 5 to 9:30 a.m. at an athletic club, washing towels and folding clothes. Then he went to classes—the school did pay for his undergraduate studies—before reporting to the basketball office, where he worked late into the night. His wife had graduated by this time, and she worked to support them.

Then came a stroke of fortune. When one of the assistant coaches had a falling-out with the head coach, Schertz, though technically still a lowly G. A., got all of the assistant's responsibilities, including scouting. At the age of twenty-two, he got a crash course in the coaching business.

At the end of that year, however, Florida Atlantic cleaned house in its basketball department, firing head coach Kevin Billerman and all of his assistants ("They gave them a couple of hours to clear out," Schertz recalls) except one. They also spared Schertz, for the time being.

"I *was* kind of a peon," he says.

When the new head coach (Sidney Green, who'd played with Michael Jordan in Chicago) came in, he scheduled an interview. Schertz showed up on time, at 9 a.m., wearing the one suit he owned, his one-page resume in hand.

"He (Green) ducked in about 6 that evening. He said he had some player meetings to take care of, and told me to wait. We met about 10 that night.

"He said that some of the players had written letters on my behalf, asking that they retain me. That wasn't a good sign, he told me, because all those guys were losers."

So Schertz ended up as part of the housecleaning. As he puts it:

"I got fired from an unpaid job."

CHAPTER 2

FROM ASSISTS TO ASSISTANT

As a kid, Josh Schertz was on the fast track to a pro career, in another sport with a net. At the age of twelve, he was one of the top-ranked junior tennis players in the country.

"From the age of two, I played tennis," he says. "I flew all over the country, playing in tournaments."

He was used to the peripatetic life. In the space of less than a decade, he and his family moved from Brooklyn, where Josh was born, to Montauk, Long Island, to Stony Brook (Long Island), and then to Coral Springs, Florida. His dad wanted him to be as serious tennis player, which was part of the reason for the move to a warmer climate.

Unfortunately, the age of twelve was also when he reached his peak as a player.

"I didn't grow," he says, "and size matters. So I was good, but not elite."

At age fifteen he was done with tennis. "I didn't enjoy it anymore," he says. "I was in a weird place." It was then that he picked up a basketball.

"I wasn't allowed to play other sports before that. Then I started playing basketball, and really enjoyed it. It was something I could do by myself. I had good motor skills, and I picked it up quickly. Then I started really working on my game. I'd shoot for hours.

"I also liked the team concept of basketball. In tennis, you can't contribute if you're playing badly. In basketball, if you're not doing one thing well, you can still do something else to help the team."

"You must immerse yourself in the selfish development of your own skills, and then put those skills to use in the context of playing with four other guys."

Those are the words of Pete Carril, the former Princeton coach, in his book, *The Smart Take from the Strong*. Carril was considered a basketball guru for his "Princeton offense," which sought to maximize, by perfectly sublimating, individual skills to team efficiency. I got to see the famous offense close-up, during the six games we played (four of them losses) against Princeton over the three years of my college career.

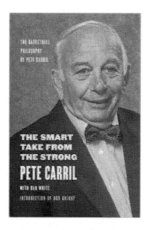

Princeton's strategy on offense was to screen-and-roll (back then that's what it was called, before *pick*-and-roll) and back-door you to death, make at least 112 passes per possession, and end up with a layup. (Keep in mind that this was also before the shot clock.) Sometimes it seemed like an opposing team's (ours included) attitude was something on the order of, *All right, already, go ahead and score, so that we can play with the ball for a while.*

Carril didn't get the best athletes at Princeton, but he did get some of the smartest, so the offense (and a terrific man-to-man defense) served him well in several David-vs.-Goliath matchups over the years. In 1989, in the first round of the NCAA tournament, Princeton took Georgetown down to the wire (and got robbed on a no-call with a second left) before losing, 50-49. It would have been the only defeat ever of a number-one seed by a sixteen seed. In 1996, Carril's last season at Princeton, his team beat UCLA, the defending national champion, in the tournament's first round, 43-41. The sight of the rumpled, often bow-tied and always un-photogenic Carril, prowling the sidelines, wearing his emotions on his sleeve, made him a popular postseason figure, and the Tigers a sentimental choice in a game against whatever major power they were matched up with in the tournament.

Carril flourished at Princeton for three decades (he is the only coach to win 500 games without the luxury of athletic scholarships), with a system he succinctly characterized in the book he wrote in 1997, a year after he'd left Princeton for a coaching job in the NBA:

"You try to put a player in a situation where those things he does well can occur."

Like Pete Carril, Josh Schertz was an undersized but over-achieving player. He loved the game, but he had no notion that he could play it in college. But he did, even if it took some bouncing around: He went from a junior college in New Jersey, to an NAIA school in Florida, to Webber after a year off, and then on to Piedmont. In the end, his determination to be a coach was nudged along by something else besides Feinstein's book.

"If I had been a better player, I would have enjoyed playing more," he says.

After the unceremonious fall of the ax at Florida Atlantic, Schertz was the beneficiary of some calls on his behalf by the boss also out on his ear, Kevin Billerman (a former Dukie). He got interviews at three places. One of them was at Lynn University, for an assistant's job. It was the job he wanted, as Lynn was just a mile down the road from Florida Atlantic. At first, though, Lynn didn't want him, so when one of the other schools, Florida Southern, offered him a gig as a part-time assistant, he accepted.

"I was there for a day," he says.

Lynn called him the next day, having reconsidered. They could make room for him and offer him a nominal salary. Schertz was thrilled; he could stay with his family in Boca Raton. When he called the Florida Southern coach to tell him, it didn't go over well. But at least they'd gotten something out of the short-lived relationship: Schertz brought one of the "losers" cut by Sidney Green at Florida Atlantic along with him to Florida Southern, where he signed to play on the day Schertz was there.

(NOTE: After this past season at LMU, Schertz was offered the head coaching job at Florida Southern. He accepted it—and stayed for just six hours this time. "I don't think they'll ever call me again," he says.)

At Lynn, Schertz had a great two years, even though the "nominal" salary promised turned out to be no salary at all during the first year. "I worked as a volunteer, basically," he says. "But I was able to stay home with my wife and son, and I learned a ton."

That first year, he got thrust into the thick of things right away. Lynn had hired a main assistant, but he couldn't get moved quickly enough, so that summer it was just Schertz, who was supposed to be way down on the totem pole, and the head coach. Schertz got put in charge of recruiting.

"At age 23, I was the recruiting coordinator," he says. "It was a fluky break." The head assistant arrived in September, but by the end of that season he'd moved on to administration, so Schertz retained his lofty title and hefty responsibilities.

"I was gone on the road all the time. I learned a lot about evaluating players, and at that point I was more interested in that than in the tactical side of basketball."

At the end of his first year, having finished up his studies and graduated from Florida Atlantic, Schertz was made a graduate assistant and given a stipend of $3,000. The next year, he started on his Master's, at Lynn. In June following that season, he was on his way to a camp at the University of Florida, when he got a call from the head coach at Queens University in Charlotte. A friend of him had recommended him as the best recruiter in Florida. He was offered $12,000, plus room and board, to sign on as an assistant—a huge jump from $3,000 a year, with no perks. And he'd be able to finish up his Master's online.

Over his two years at Lynn, the Fighting Knights went 37-18; Schertz's lasting legacy was the five-man recruiting class he signed in 2001, which went on to lead Lynn to a school-record 29 wins and a Final Four appearance in 2005. Four players he signed made All-Conference. Early on, he was showing a sharp eye for talent.

CHAPTER 3

WILL AN ITCH LEAD TO A NICHE?

As the new millennium began, with Dean Smith and Pete Carril long gone from the college game, Josh Schertz was a young coach on the rise. Having gotten the call from head coach Bart Lundy at Queens, Schertz drove to Charlotte and went right to work as Lundy's assistant.

After his first season at Queens, Schertz was promoted to associate head coach, an impressive title without any additional money involved. "Sort of like throwing a dog a bone," Schertz says, but it did show that Lundy wanted to keep him around. For good reason, as Schertz was dogged in his pursuit of big-time players. He landed two of the biggest-time – Spencer Ross, who was 2004 National Division II Player of the Year, and another All-American, Moustapha Diouf.

In 2003, Schertz's second year at Queens, the Royals won a school-record 29 games and went to the Final Four, losing to the eventual national champions. After that landmark season, Bart Lundy got hired at High Point (North Carolina). He asked Schertz to come with him, but Schertz wanted the head coach's job at Queens, and many of the players wanted him to get it.

Schertz wanted the head coach's job at Queens, but it wasn't to be

He went to see the athletic director. She told him she wouldn't hire him. Why not? he wanted to know -- I'm a known quantity, so you've got no risk involved. If I succeed, great; if I don't, you can just let me go. The A. D. said that Queens would always be a Final Four-caliber team, and it had nothing to do with Schertz.

"It was smart of them not to hire me," he says. "I wasn't ready for the job."

He didn't know – or wouldn't admit – that then, however, and, in contrast with Dean Smith, who was reluctant to take the job as North Carolina's head man in 1961, at the age of 30, Schertz was *itching* to be a head coach.

Having been shot down by Queens' queen of athletics, Schertz packed up and drove with Bart Lundy to High Point. He spent a year there as Lundy's assistant, then was promoted again to associate head coach, a position he held for the next five years. The Panthers went 87-66 in that span, establishing school records for wins and highest RPI rating.

Schertz also served as the program's recruiting coordinator. Two of the players he landed, Danny Gathings and Arizona Reid, turned out to be Big South Player of the Year (Reid was honored twice), and he also signed 2,000 point-scorer Nick Barbour, all-time assist leader Mike Jefferson, and all-time shot-blocker Cruz Daniels.

While High Point was going places, Schertz was getting nowhere in his quest for a head coaching gig. When there were openings that appealed to him, he applied, but no one was interested.

"I wasn't unhappy (at High Point), but I wanted to see what I could do on my own," he says.

When the LMU job opened up, he sent his stuff in, and then called. A. D. Roger Vannoy happened to answer. He and Schertz chatted for a while, and Vannoy seemed interested. Later, Bart Lundy called on Schertz's behalf. ("He didn't think I'd take the job," Schertz says.)

Schertz went up for a visit and interview. There were four or five candidates, he recalls, and he was the second one to interview. He was offered the job on the spot. This was on a Tuesday; he told them he needed some time, and said he'd let them know Friday.

Schertz was also in the running for the head coach's position at UNC Pembroke. It paid more, but Schertz preferred LMU, even though he'd also be taking a pay cut to leave High Point for there. He decided to cancel his interview at Pembroke, and signed on with Lincoln.

High Point came back with an offer of $12,000 more to stay on. Now, he'd be making $25,000 less at LMU.

"I called Roger back on Friday to tell him," Schertz says. "He was real nice about it. He gave me until Sunday to make up my mind."

He spent a miserable weekend. He met with the A. D. and the president of High Point. "The vibe I got," he says, "was that I should go." On Sunday, he called Vannoy to tell him he was coming.

Schertz drove from High Point to Harrogate on a Monday in late March, accompanied by his wife and child and by his first hire, Chris Cottrell, whom he'd plucked from the High Point staff to be his assistant. He had no grandiose expectations, nor did his new bosses at Lincoln Memorial. But what he found made *any* expectations seem grandiose.

Schertz and Cottrell had scheduled meetings and workouts with the individual returning players on Tuesday. "It was a fiasco," Schertz recalls. "I knew it would be bad, but the level of disarray was beyond belief. There were guys who missed their meetings, guys who were asleep when we went to look for them."

There were six scholarship players, and none of them could play, as was made manifest during the workouts. And there was money tied up in them for years.

There was a press conference scheduled for Wednesday. At the end of the day Tuesday, Schertz told Cottrell, "We're going back to High Point. There's no way we can win here." He told his wife the same thing--that he was in over his head here—but assured her that Bart Lundy was holding his spot, knowing that this was how it would turn out.

He called Lundy, who didn't pick up. In the three hours that it took Lundy to return his call, Schertz convinced himself to stay—sort of. Getting ready for the press conference the next day, he told Cottrell again, "You know, we can just get in the car and drive back." The LMU people wanted him to wear a logo tie for the event; his wife told him, "You're not wearing that thing."

He went through with the press conference, and plugged it out afterwards. He, Cottrell, and Lance Egnatz, another new hire in his first full-time job, stayed in three apartments side by side for the next six months -or just slept there, actually, while making the fieldhouse their home. (Schertz's wife and son had returned to North Carolina.)

Schertz flanked by assistants Chris Cottrell and Lance Egnatz

"We'd work from 7 a.m. until past midnight every day, then hit the Waffle King (in nearby Middleboro) before passing out," Schertz says.

They had a plan, one which was in accord with Roger Vannoy's modest hopes for the program, which were, in a nutshell, to get rid of the riffraff, get on an even keel, and get things pointed in the right direction. For this, he was giving Schertz four years.

This plan involved, first and foremost, testing everyone's mettle, which is a nice way of saying: trying to run people off. "None of them had come there to play for me," says Schertz. "And some of them couldn't adapt to the new culture." The two best players quit within two weeks. They didn't like having to be at breakfast early every morning. They didn't like study halls. They didn't like the workouts. When the smoke cleared, three were left standing: Ryan Whitaker, Wadner Joseph, and Matt Bogard.

"It was a good thing, the original group scattering," says Schertz. "If they'd stayed, it would have slowed down our growth."

In a way, Schertz was lucky that first year. He was hired on March 22, which gave him and his staff four full months to recruit. (Schertz made Egnatz his recruiting coordinator.) And scholarship money had been freed up, what with the players jumping ship. Between April 1 and the end of July, nine new scholarship players were added to the roster, plus six more as walk-ons.

"We were worried about attrition, so we went for the overkill," Schertz says.

With that hodgepodge group, Lincoln Memorial finished the season 14-14 in all games, 8-8 in the conference. (The year before, they'd gone 8-20, 1-13.) In conference play they were 0-4 in overtime games; they also lost another, non-conference game in OT. They beat conference foe Catawba, ranked 9th in the country at the time, by 15 at home (with Catawba's coach being tossed from the game). The eight South Atlantic Conference wins were a school record, and the 14 overall wins were the most in a season since 2002-03.

"We couldn't win the close ones," Schertz says, "but we competed our tails off."

The Railsplitters lost in the first round of the conference tournament, but they had served notice: the times they were a-changin' in Harrogate.

LMU's 2008-09 team finished 14-14

SCOTT ERLAND: *"It was a weird year. A lot of times, we'd get down by 16-0 or 21-1 or something like that, but we'd always come back. We had a bunch of players who were all new to college ball, and they got a lot of experience. And in time we all came to trust and appreciate the nucleus of veterans (Bogard, Whitaker and Joseph).*

"We announced to the conference that we were for real."

CHAPTER 4

A PLATEAU REACHED – TWENTY WINS

Five or six times during that first year, Coach Schertz kicked the entire team out of practice, and had them all come back later that night to take it from the top. It wasn't for screwing anything up in particular, but for an overall lack of effort.

"You're ----ing around with my livelihood," he told them on one such occasion. "You're threatening the well-being of my family. If I have to, I'll get rid of all of you and start over."

In retrospect, Schertz says, he was never more proud of a team of his. Despite all it had going against it – a first-time head coach, fifteen brand-new players and only three experienced ones from a twenty-loss season—it resurrected LMU basketball. The fact was, had the team won, rather than lost, all of its overtime games, it would have won the conference by two full games.

Wadner Joseph, one of only three holdovers from 2007-08

"They made up for what they lacked in talent and experience with effort, toughness and attitude," Schertz says. "I drove those guys mercilessly -- way too hard -- but they never complained (at least to me)."

SCOTT ERLAND: *"It's amazing he didn't blow up at us more than he did. "We had a lot of immaturity issues."*

The second year, there were no such explosive incidents. Schertz's system was falling into place, and the players were buying into it. Whereas practices during the first season had been extremely long, now they were becoming streamlined. They still conformed to Schertz's obsession with covering every little detail, making sure that his players were prepared for anything, but the process was growing more efficient.

That's not to say that the players were mere cogs in a machine.

SCOTT E.: *"Coach Schertz was always having individual meetings. He was always telling you exactly where you stood. He was so honest that if you had a problem with him, it was likely because of yourself. He told you the truth."*

My experience with my son Scott's coaches before Josh Schertz had been often frustrating and sometimes infuriating. In Scott's eighth-grade year, his baseball coach called me up six weeks or so before the season and told me to start working Scott out, as he was counting on him to be one of the mainstays of his pitching staff. I did, but then Scott was one of the few kids on the team who *didn't* get a turn on the mound all season.

His ninth-grade basketball coach put Scott in for sixteen seconds one time, before taking him back out, and his high-school coach did him one better with an eleven-second stint. I chafed to see Scott consigned to the end of the bench as a sophomore, largely due to, as I saw it, the coach's policy of playing seniors above others, even though they might be inferior players or, even worse, indifferent as to whether they played or not. These guys had no future in the game past high school, whereas my son, obviously, was a singular talent, one languishing on the bench because of his coach's short-sightedness. (There was a kernel of truth to this, the familiar lament of the purblind parent, as it turned out that Scott *did* have a future in basketball.)

In the case of my daughter, who also played basketball in high school and then in college, her high-school coach told me the first time I ever met him that Emily, a sophomore, would definitely play ahead of another girl at her position who was only a freshman; when the opposite turned out to be the case, this worm became my sworn enemy for the next three years.

Maybe I was, indeed, deluded, and my kids weren't always good enough to play. The point is: often, neither of them knew *where they stood* with their coaches.

One of the walk-ons in year one of Schertz's tenure was an unusual one. D'Mario Curry was a six-eight talent with a sketchy background. Schertz recalls that he might have played a year of junior-college ball somewhere, but that then he was without a team for a while.

"Rusty Peace (LMU's Sports Media and Marketing Director) got a call from a guy in Detroit, who said he had a player for us," Schertz recalls. "We had no scholarship money, but Rusty said it wouldn't hurt to call him back. So I did, and I told him we appreciated it, but we didn't have anything to give the guy. He told me that was okay, he'd come as a walk-on. That raised a red flag, but we needed bodies, especially six-eight ones, so I said to send him along.

"He also said that no one had been able to coach this kid. Being young and naïve, I believed I could coach anybody. I told him it wouldn't be a problem."

Curry took a bus in from Detroit, and one of the players picked him up in Knoxville. When Schertz met him, he thought: *he won't last a week in this town.*

DeMario Curry was as good as any D2 player in the country

"Rio" made it through three years in Harrogate, and gave LMU fans, coaches and fellow players the ride of their lives. "At thirty-percent capacity, he was still one of the very best players in the country," says Schertz. "On the nights he wanted to play, we weren't going to get beat by anyone in Division 2."

Unfortunately, perhaps, the thirty percent was closer to Curry's norm. But on those occasions when he did come to play, everyone could count on seeing something they'd maybe never seen before.

** ** ** ** ** ** ** **

'Rio: An Appreciation
by Scott Erland

When I was playing, we started the majority of our practices with some type of 1-on-1 defensive drill. Drawing 'Rio as an opponent on a day when he was locked in was the worst form of psychological and physical punishment that could fall your way. I'll never forget the day I received that honor.

I was matched up against 'Rio in a full-court, 1-on-1 drill. In this particular drill, if the offensive player scored, he maintained possession and got a point. If the defensive player got a stop, he took over on offense. The loser had to run a couple of sprints, while the winner watched from the sideline while enjoying some water. I never touched the ball *one time* offensively. After Rio thoroughly and completely humiliated me in seven or eight straight trips down the floor, I looked at Coach Egnatz and said, "Nobody in the country could stop him right now." All he could do was smile and nod his head.

This really happened:

In a 5-on-5 drill at the end of practice, 'Rio caught the ball on a fast break, leapt over Brandon Armstrong (former LMU guard and now a social-media sensation), and flushed a one-handed dunk that left everybody stunned. Let me reiterate: he actually jumped OVER Brandon. Hardly anyone even remarked on it, though, because things of that nature were more or less commonplace with Rio.

The Great Demoralizer:

During a preseason workout in preparation for Coach Schertz's first season, 'Rio was absolutely demolishing a weary walk-on, who will be known as Charles, in a closeout drill. After five or six straight humiliating defensive stands, Charles halfheartedly "closed out" on 'Rio, who picked up a full head of steam and viciously dunked it, knocking Charles to the ground in the process. In response, Charles walked off the court, took off his shoes and told Coach Schertz he was done. He actually quit the team after 'Rio dunked on him.

A game against Catawba:

I think everybody just accepted the fact that 'Rio was probably the most talented player in Division II. He didn't show that all of the time, or even come close to reaching his potential as a player, but he would occasionally have games that you knew would be stamped in your mind forever. One of those in particular was a game against Catawba during his senior season. He put up 30 points and 12 rebounds in the *first half*.

There was a group of younger kids that sat in the bleachers under one of the baskets, and they made up a unique sort of cheering section. In the first half, Rio stole the ball, drove down and dunked in some hapless guy's face; to add insult to injury, the guy got whistled for a foul. 'Rio's kids went nuts; I'll never forget watching 'Rio hand out high-fives to all of them before draining the free throw.

He finished with a modest 41 points and 21 rebounds. Oh, and he added seven assists. That's the kind of thing he was capable of on a nightly basis.

Vols victimized:

'Rio scored 24 points against Tennessee in an exhibition before the 2009-10 season. That was the year they went to the Elite Eight, losing in the regional finals. They knew 'Rio was the only player that could hurt them, and he still had his way against those guys.

** ** ** ** ** ** ** **

In 2009-10, Lincoln Memorial, led by Curry, posted its first-ever 20-win season at the Division II level. The team had added four new players (among them future mainstays Cam Carden, Wally Jones and Dustin Craig) and had almost every rotation player back from the year before, including seniors Bogard and Joseph. None of the players were ones that Schertz and his staff hadn't recruited themselves. The Railsplitters, settling a little into Schertz's system, were much more consistent, and it helped that Curry turned into a monster, averaging 17 a game and 11 rebounds while delivering his usual quotient of eye-popping plays.

Cam Carden (l) and Dustin Craig

LMU came out like gangbusters, starting the season 10-1 and getting to 17-3 before fading down the stretch, losing five of its last eight. Four of those five losses were heart-breakers, Schertz recalls, all of them resolved at or near the buzzer, with LMU losing late-game advantages. The Railsplitters had a chance to win the league, sitting in first place with two games to go, but they lost leads inside the final five seconds to Carson Newman and Newberry, and finished fourth.

LMU beat Mars Hill at home in the first round of SAC tournament, its first-ever postseason win, and headed to Hickory, NC, for the semifinal round of play. Schertz calls the three days of the conference tournament that year the most difficult of his life. The Railsplitters were ranked number seven in the region heading into the semis, but lost by ten to Catawba on Saturday; the next day, they watched as Brevard upset Catawba for the SAC championship, and when USC Aiken upset Montevallo for the Peachbelt championship, LMU was knocked out of the NCAA Tournament.

As Schertz drove home from Hickory with his family, he was consoled and counseled by his grandfather, who up to that point had been the most important person in his life. His grandfather passed away the next day.

CHAPTER 5

PRACTICING FOR PERFECTION

On the day of my son Scott's first college basketball game, I got a call from him, saying he was starting that night. I hadn't allowed for such a possibility – Scott was a walk-on, after all – so I had to drop what I was doing and hightail it for Harrogate, a four-hour drive for a cautious (that is to say, *semi-elderly*) driver like me.

I'd heard of, and even had, coaches who told their troops that they'd all have an equal opportunity to play. This was always, in my experience, so much "motivational" hot air. But here was one coach, I marveled on my way to LMU, who actually put his money where his mouth was.

SCOTT ERLAND: *"You can always get in Coach Schertz's good graces if you practice hard."*

"When I played at Webber, I was the backup point guard, period," Schertz explains. "The starting lineup was set in stone in October, and barring death or disabling injury, you were starting – there was no chance for someone to jump ahead of you. That created a lethargic attitude at practices – what was the use of going hard if you couldn't work your way into the starting lineup?

"I decided I'd do it differently when I got to be a head coach. My policy is, if you practice well, you'll get an opportunity to start.

"Last year (2014-15), ten different guys got to start. All of them earned it. If you earn it, you'll get it, no matter who you are."

Schertz says there's another reason for leaving the starting lineup an open issue, besides fostering competitive practices.

"There's no sense in being married to a starting lineup in October, or anytime, for that matter. Hardly anyone plays at a high level all season. What's clicking in October may not be in January, February or March. You make adjustments depending on who's playing well. Our guys understand that."

Beyond the question of who's starting, Schertz says he approaches the game as a whole like most other coaches.

"I allocate playing time based on what gives our team its best chance to win."

From the beginning, practices under Schertz varied from day to day, so that things didn't get stale, but everything that was done, even the smallest things, was competitive. As Coach Pete Carril used to say, competition during practice creates a little tension, so that the players get used to it in games. Each day (Monday through Saturday before the season started) began with stretching, followed by shooting. (At first, Schertz didn't insist on ankles being taped, but after a number of ankle injuries, taping became the rule.) Then came game-situation scrimmages, with the team split into two squads, and the losing squad having to run timed sprints. (Carril, from *The Smart Take from the Strong*: "Everything we do in practice has to do with something that happens in a game.") Assistant Chris Cottrell worked with the guards, Lance Egnatz the forwards.

SCOTT E.: *"I think it's difficult for a coach to keep practices fun and engaging while never diverting from the ultimate goal of individual and team development. Schertz managed to do that, though, because everything was competitive, and you ultimately knew that how well you performed in practice mattered. We practiced incredibly hard, but it was always with a purpose and it never turned stale."*

Of course, running was, and is, a big part of the daily routine. A favorite Schertz torture is called "Seventeens." The victims spread out along the sideline, and at the sound of the whistle must run seventeen widths of the court within a minute and ten seconds; if any one fails to do so, the whole team has to do it again.

Practices were long and grueling in Schertz's first two years, but they gradually grew shorter as the staff became more efficient in conveying information – and because Schertz saw that some players were wearing down.

SCOTT E.: *"Coach Schertz hadn't quite developed his system yet, and we hadn't adjusted our attitudes to it. Now, everything is in place; it all perpetuates itself."*

Coach Egnatz oversaw weightlifting sessions four days a week during preseason, and two or three days during the season. (Schertz was instrumental in getting a strength-and-conditioning coach put on staff at LMU prior to the 2014-15 season.) After the season started, the team watched film for twenty minutes before practice every day, either reviewing its last game or getting familiar with an upcoming opponent. The two assistants split up the scouting reports; in laying out a strategy for the next game, the principles were always the same, but tweaks were made depending on the opponent.

SCOTT E.: *"By the time January rolled around, there was a definite rhythm and structure to the week. We wrapped up the previous Saturday's game with film and started to prep for the upcoming opponent on Monday. Tuesday was entirely devoted to preparation for Wednesday's game. On game day, we would have about a two-hour walkthrough with a last look at the opponent for that night. That process started afresh on Thursday. Sunday was our only off day, and it was much-needed after a long week of practice."*

Now, the basketball staff consists of two full-time assistants (Cameron Wicker and Davis Fisher) and two graduate assistants (Jeremiah Samarrippas and Omar Wattad). The GA's are always on the court during practices, while the assistants are sometimes behind the scenes.

Lincoln Memorial's current coaching staff

In 2010-11, LMU had most of the team back from the year before, and added some crucial new pieces, including high-school recruits Vincent Bailey and Chance Jones and transfer Darryl Garrett. Schertz calls it his most talented team, one that when it was ready to play (ah, that old qualifier) was as good as any in the country.

"We had a lot of characters on that team," he recalls. "It tested us as a staff in a lot of ways, but despite our dysfunction we had guys who wanted to win."

The Railsplitters began the season by winning 22 games in a row, a school record for consecutive wins. In December, they were nationally-ranked for the first time ever. They lost their first game at

Brevard, a defeat Schertz considers as disappointing a one as he's ever had. Vinnie Bailey was out with a fracture in his foot, diagnosed just before the bus pulled off of campus, and Schertz barely played two of his other best players, for disciplinary reasons. Following the game, he suspended one of the two for the rest of the regular season. LMU lost its very next game as well, following up the 22-game winning streak with a two-game losing streak.

LMU 2010-11 team

The 'Splitters rebounded to win five straight, wrapping up their first-ever SAC regular-season title, and followed that up by winning the school's first-ever SAC Tournament title. The jubilation was short-lived, however, as second-seeded LMU was upset in the first round of the NCAA Tournament by

Anderson, who went on to win the region as a number-seven seed.

SCOTT ERLAND (who was in his first year on staff in the LMU athletic department): *"I remember I couldn't go to the (Anderson) game because I had to work a baseball game. When I announced the final score at the baseball game, there was an audible gasp. People were looking up at the press box, thinking I was fooling around."*

Actually, two of LMU's three losses that year were to Anderson. The loss in the regional spawned a bitter rivalry.

The Railsplitters' 27-3 record was the best in school history. They were undefeated at home. The team had five double-digit scorers, outscored opponents by an average of 17 points a game, and out-rebounded them by more than ten a game. LMU completely dominated its foes in every category, including assists (450 to 350), steals (240 to 185), blocked shots (96 to 66), and field-goal percentage (.495 to .392!). Desmond Johnson was named SAC Player of the Year, and D'Mario Curry was also named first-team All-SAC for the third year in a row.

Desmond Johnson

"I'll always be proud of what that team accomplished," says Schertz. "But because of its level of talent, I'll always be sad about what we left on the table, due to self-imposed obstacles."

CHAPTER 6

CHARACTER, NOT CHARACTERS

Josh Schertz is one coach who likes recruiting, though not as much as he used to.

"I enjoy getting to know kids and their families," he says. "What I don't enjoy is when some people don't have the kids' best interests at heart."

Recruiting is a year-round process, and involves a great deal of intensive research. Schertz and his staff look carefully at every kid they're interested in, with an eye toward assessing talent, of course, but also judging the "intangibles" – fiber, character, coachability – what, and who, the kid *is*.

"We try to get as much intelligence as we can," says Schertz, which is not to imply that recruiting is like spying -- or not exactly.

"We'll try to get game film to start with. My assistants will watch it first, and if they like the kid, I'll watch it then. Talent is the first criterion.

"If the talent's there, we'll talk to the kid's high-school and AAU coaches. How does he practice? How does he interact with his teammates? When we can, we'll watch a practice. How does he take coaching? How does he carry himself?

"We'll talk to rival coaches. Scouting services are a big help.

"How is the kid academically? We'll talk to his principal, and to his teachers if we can.

"When we get serious, then we'll talk to the kid himself."

Coach Schertz on the electronic recruiting trail

Schertz and his assistants are usually gone almost the entire month of July, when AAU tournaments are hot and heavy. It's at these events where they can see prospects *en masse*.

Once they've identified a player as a desirable recruit, they'll add him to their list, which is divided up, color-coded and alphabetized by position and priority (A, B, C and below). They (the assistants) will go over the list twice a week; each Sunday, Schertz will get a "hot list" of prospects to call, or to call about.

LMU recruits for basketball mostly within a five-hour radius, which encompasses all or parts of eight states, including the hotbeds of Indiana, Kentucky and Ohio. That's a lot of ground to cover, and a lot of players to try and see, and a lot of intelligence to be had. If, in this electronic day and age, information-gathering is more viable, then it's also more crucial to analyze the information gathered. As Schertz says:

"One bad apple can spoil what we're trying to do."

A recruiting story: When I was a senior in high school, Lefty Driesell was the coach at Davidson. (He was to leave the next year for Maryland, where he would lock horns with Dean Smith, both on the court and verbally, for seventeen years.) When Davidson came to Nashville to play Vanderbilt, Lefty invited me and my mom to attend the game and sit behind his bench.

Lefty Driesell

Davidson was ranked in the top five in the country at the time, and Vandy was in the top ten. The game was close. Lefty had been riding the referees all night. My mom was half-amused, half-offended by the foot-stomping and salty language he was steadily employing, either to get the refs' attention or to berate one of his players. I told her it was typical Lefty, from what I'd heard.

With about a minute to go in the tight game, a fifth foul was called on Mike Malloy, Davidson's All-American. Lefty erupted, and stormed onto the court. The head referee T'd him up. Lefty blew his top, unleashing a stream of invectives we could hear even above the roar of the crowd. The ref gave him a second technical.

Lefty was now apoplectic. The refs were waving him off the floor, but he refused to go. He was at half-court, whirling, flapping his arms and squawking like a chicken in its death throes. The refs threatened to forfeit the game, I think. Still, Lefty wouldn't leave. There was pandemonium in Memorial Gym.

Finally, one of the refs went to the sideline and summoned a security guard. The game came onto the court, took Lefty by the arm and led him forcefully into the locker room, to the mingled, hoots, howls and applause of the crowd. Vanderbilt got four free throws and possession of the ball, and ended up winning the game. When my mom was able to make herself heard above the din, she said:

"There's no way on Earth you're going to play for that man."

Character counts, in a coach as well as a player.

SCOTT ERLAND: *"Coach Schertz was always able to balance the way he treated you on the court with how he treated you off of it – his personal relationships with his authority. He created a family atmosphere from the beginning – it was crazy how fast he created that. You could always go and talk to him about personal stuff. You could see that he genuinely cared about you as a person. It wasn't fake.*

"At the same time, he had that authority. You could feel it in the way he carried himself. Everyone both liked and respected him. You knew you were lucky to be coached by him."

Sometimes, character can even eclipse talent. Wally Jones, who came to Lincoln Memorial in 2009 and played for four years, is a case in point.

"Wally was a borderline college player in high school," Schertz says. "He was going to Division 3, probably. When I met him, I was intrigued by him and his family. If I had judged him on basketball alone, I wouldn't have signed him. But I could see what a great character he had."

Wally Jones

Jones started only seven, six and nine games his first three years at LMU, but in his senior year he started 25 at guard, averaging 10.9 points a game, third-best on the team. Over his four-year career the Railsplitters went 98-24 and won three straight South Atlantic Conference titles.

SCOTT E.: *"Wally was one of the nicest, most genuine people I've ever had the pleasure of playing with. Everybody loved him as a person and admired his absurd dedication to his fitness and game. I think Wally pulled other players along and made everyone want to be a better version of themselves.*

"I would be remiss if I didn't mention how sad the end of his career was. He missed some time for a new injury during his junior year and he blew out his knee again in one of the final regular season games his senior year. He never sulked or felt sorry for himself. I remember really admiring the way he acted after that injury."

If Schertz sometimes makes decisions based on issues of character, it's not for any holier-than-thou reasons, he says, but for the good of the team. As he points out, the best *teams* usually win, not necessarily the best players.

That's another reason he enjoys recruiting. "You're trying to build a team – trying to put the pieces of a puzzle together," he says.

Schertz admires what coach Steve Kerr did this season in the NBA, molding a group that was outstanding the year before into something truly special. Golden State had a couple of All-Stars coming off the bench, and everyone contributed to the 67-win campaign, the seventh-best in league history. In the NBA Finals, the Warriors fell behind in games 2-1 to the Cavaliers and the league's best player, whereupon Kerr inserted Andre Iguodala into the starting lineup. Iguodala, who hadn't started a game all season, harassed LeBron James into a subpar performance in Game 4, a 21-point Warriors win, which turned the series around.

When the dust had settled, the best *team* had won.

CHAPTER 7

"IT'S JUST WHAT HE DOES"

At the end of his third year at Lincoln Memorial, with a monumental 27-3 record under his belt, having been named the South Atlantic Conference Coach of the Year and pegged as one of the finalists for Division II National Coach of the Year, Josh Schertz...couldn't have been more miserable.

"Even though we started off 22-0, we had to suspend some guys," he says. "We had to reset the program. I wanted to win, but not at all costs."

That win-with-honor resolve was shared by Schertz's biggest and most steadfast supporter, Autry O. V. (Pete) DeBusk, Chairman of the LMU Board of Trustees. A year earlier, DeBusk had stepped in when Schertz had an opportunity to leave LMU for another, higher paying coaching position, and had wooed him back into the fold with a substantial raise.

From that point on, DeBusk's involvement was "hot and heavy," Schertz says.

Pete DeBusk

In 2011-12, LMU began the season ranked second in the national polls. The Railsplitters came out of the gate on fire again, winning fifteen in a row to start. On January 10, 2012, Lincoln Memorial was ranked number one in the country for the first time in school history. From that point on, the team went 11-6, dropping two games to Carson Newman and two games to Anderson, and finishing second in the league. The 'Splitters lost in the semifinals of the SAC tournament, but made it into the NCAA regional tournament as a four seed.

There, LMU won its first-ever NCAA Tournament game (March 10, 2012) against King College (now King University). In the next round, against tournament host Montevallo, the Railsplitters had a 14-point lead with eight minutes to go. Montevallo came back, and won the game with a wild, running hook shot off the backboard with two seconds to go, 61-60.

The loss was gut-wrenching, and made worse by the fact that Montevallo made it all the way to the national championship game. Schertz calls it unquestionably the toughest loss of his tenure at LMU.

SCOTT ERLAND: *"An opinion shared by many close to the men's hoops program: I thought I was going to be sick after the final buzzer sounded. I watched the entire thing via live stream from my office, and the last eight minutes were horrific. I'll never forget it."*

Vinnie Bailey

Besides the number-one ranking, the season was notable for the emergence of sophomore Vinnie Bailey as the Railsplitters' best player (he was named All-SAC second team, while Desmond Johnson and Brandon Armstrong made the first team), for the consistent play of newcomer Jake Troyli, and for the debut of another budding star, Lorenza Ross.

That year, sporting its gaudy 15-0 record, the Railsplitters had gone on the road to play Anderson. LMU was up by 18 in the second half, when Anderson switched its defense to a 1-3-1 zone. Schertz stuck with the players who had built the big lead, despite the fact that none of them were particularly good shooters. Anderson came back and won the game in overtime.

"I cost us the game," Schertz says. "I didn't have the right guys on the floor. We lost because of my inability to adjust."

He says he's much better at it now, but he's still learning.

"There are so many little decisions to be made in a game. When to adjust what you're doing as a team is the hardest one."

Substitutions and changes in pace of play are a couple of obvious varieties of adjustments, but many more are not noticeable to the average spectator, Schertz notes.

"The other team's making tough shots – do we scrap what we're doing or stay with it?

"We're having trouble scoring – do we 'go small,' and spread the floor, or stay 'big' and be more aggressive?

"Do we double the post on defense? Do we change how we're coping with screens?

"I call a time-out. What message do they need now? Do I jump them, or stay calm?"

Coach Schertz considers his options

Schertz wonders if he over-adjusted in LMU's upset loss to Mt. Olive in last year's opening round of the regional tournament. Mt. Olive went with two big guys and jumped out to a big lead; Schertz switched to a smaller lineup, but it didn't help – the hole got deeper. Did he make a change too soon?

He wonders, but he doesn't dwell on it, if he can help it.

"I'm self-critical, but I try to put things behind me," he says. "I try not to let a game beat me twice."

That's why, four years later now, he only thinks about that Montevallo game once a week or so.

Details are what wins or loses games," Schertz says, which explains why he's an obsessive – there are always more details to go over. During the season, he'll put in over 100 hours a week at it – in the off-season, only 80 or so.

"You always feel a sense of urgency to catch up with things, to figure out what you need to do," he says. "That never changes; I feel it as much as I ever have. I understand it better, I have a little better perspective, but the urgency is still there.

"I'll be on vacation in Florida (for a week during the summer), and most of the time I'll be thinking about the team. You can never really get away from it.

"This is more of a lifestyle than a job. You don't punch in and punch out."

Each off-season, Schertz and staff will thoroughly study each loss from the previous season, as well as those games, or stretches of games, when the team didn't play well. (This summer, they went over every possession of last season's two *wins* over Catawba, to try and understand why that particular foe gave them relative fits.) Last year's team, Schertz says, was better in February than it was in mid-March. So he's spent a good part of this summer trying to figure out why.

"There's really no off-season," he says. "There's no rest. But I like that."

As for the players, they get two weeks off when the season ends. Then they come back for weight training, supervised by the assistant coaches. Schertz is hands-off in this, which he says is a good thing for everyone concerned.

"The last thing they need to hear in the off-season is me yelling at them," he says. "They need a break from me." Schertz looks at it as "repair time" – an opportunity for mending the relationships that may have been frayed over the previous season. The only conversations, or contacts, he'll have with players are non-basketball ones. Spring and summer, as he sees it, is the time to build the rapport that will allow him to push his players during the long season to come.

"The freshmen are happy as clams now," Schertz says, on this fair day in June. "Whenever they see me, I'll be happy-go-lucky. They think I'm the nicest guy in the world.

"In August, it all flips."

August is when the season starts in earnest, with conditioning drills and scrimmaging and team meetings – and when the real challenge begins for Schertz and his staff: taking a group that's not yet a team and making it into one. Few people recognize how difficult a process that is.

SCOTT ERLAND: *"The most impressive thing about Coach Schertz is that every year he has massive question marks about what he has left for the coming season. After 2010-11, for example, Curry and Garrett (30* points a game combined) were gone, and the next year different guys stepped up or changed roles, and Vinnie became the player we thought he'd be. We were 26-6.

"After 2012, Desmond was gone, but Lorenza, Wally and Cam (Carden) stepped up. We went 25-6.

"Then, in 2014, we lost Vinnie and Chance Jones – 37 points a game from two seniors. I didn't think we'd be any good at all the next year, but we didn't miss a beat. We won 30 games!

"Every single year he (Schertz) faces the same dilemmas, and every year he figures it out. It's unbelievable. But it's just what he does."

CHAPTER 8

COACHES: THICK AS THIEVES?

There are any number of coaches, both pro and college, past and present, whom Josh Schertz admires, among them Greg Popovich ("the best at any level"), Steve Kerr and Brett Brown (of the Philadelphia 76'ers – "he handles failure well") in the NBA; Bill Self (Kansas), Bo Ryan (Wisconsin) and Rick Pitino in the college ranks; and Billy Donovan and Brad Stevens, who have made, or are making, the transition from college to the pros.

He marvels at Kentucky's John Calipari's ability to recruit. "That's a big part of it," he says. "He's head and shoulders above anyone else." Schertz also concedes that Calipari does an underappreciated job of getting everyone to play together.

Are there college coaches he doesn't care for?

"Anyone who thinks it's all about them," he says. "I'm not dumb enough to think so."

Growing up, he liked Jeff Van Gundy, coach of the New York Knicks and then the Houston Rockets in the NBA. ("He was a little guy who didn't look the part.") Schertz says he's not a huge NBA fan, but that he watches pro games to try and learn.

Jeff Van Gundy

"I don't look at it as a fan, but as a coach. I admire the players who work at it and compete – Tim Duncan, for example, who continues to grind it out even though he's had all that success and doesn't need the money – and I appreciate different coaches for how they do things."

Schertz says he'd like to be the genteel, even-keeled type of coach, like the Celtics' Brad Stevens, but that it wouldn't be true to his personality. "I gotta be me," he says. The persona that LMU players and fans have grown to know and love (sort of) is one strongly given over to sarcasm.

SCOTT ERLAND: *"Coach Schertz isn't the type to blow up. He hardly ever gets irate, but he's always sarcastic."*

Sarcasm, for Schertz, is a vent for his anger. "I might take a guy out of a game," he says, "and under my breath I'll say something like, 'I guess I can't play you tonight, since you can't guard anybody.'"

SCOTT E.: *"We were getting stomped in a Saturday afternoon game at Virginia-Wise during Coach Schertz's first season. This seems unbelievable now, as we regularly bash UVA-Wise by 40 or 50 points, but at that point we were a young and inconsistent bunch. Nothing was going well for us, especially at the free throw line. On one occasion in the second half, Brandon Armstrong was at the charity stripe. As soon as the ball left his hand, Schertz yelled out, 'Nice try, B.A. Get back on defense.' Brandon's shot rim out and the small crowd had a laugh at our misfortunes and Coach Schertz's sarcasm."*

Since there are 15 or 16 different personalities on a team, you have to coach them to *your* personality, Schertz says.

"I won't coddle them, or blow smoke," he says. "They have to get over themselves. They have to be able to take the sarcasm, the yelling. It's never demeaning or embarrassing or in their face – I don't challenge their intellect. But I do demand a lot of them.

"Not everybody can play for me."

Schertz says he's friendly with most coaches he competes against, and that he has "good relationships" with the other coaches in the conference.

"It can be harder when you see each other so often," he says, "but in a way you develop a respect for each other and you can become really good friends. With (Coach) Chuck Benson at Carson Newman, for example, there's a huge rivalry. Our fans hate him and their team, but he and I get along fine. I don't take our competition personally. I don't get mad at him if they beat us.

"You're pretty small if you can't be happy for someone else's success."

That attitude is a far cry from the sniping, infighting, jealousies and resentments described by

John Feinstein in his book about the ACC and its coaches, back in the mid-'70s. All the other coaches resented Dean Smith, whose perceived aloofness Feinstein ascribed to shyness; all of them agreed, to one degree or another, that there was a "double standard" when it came to North Carolina's teams and the referees. The bickering took the form of snubbing, caustic comments to the press, shouting matches, and on at least one occasion, a near-physical confrontation, between Smith and Coach Rick Barnes, in his first year at Clemson.

Such animosity, to him, Schertz says, would be counter-productive:

"I've got my own team to worry about."

Going into the 2012-13, season, Schertz had plenty to worry about. The Railsplitters weren't picked to win the league, as they had lost two first-team all-conference players in Desmond Johnson and Brandon Armstrong. And the team struggled through the first two-thirds of the schedule, even though it was a veteran group that had won a lot. As Schertz puts it:

"We were fighting human nature as it relates to complacency."

The low point of the season, and its turning point, was when Newberry came to town, rang up 113 points and embarrassed the Railsplitters on their home floor. (SCOTT ERLAND: *"I'll also never forget that game. Newberry hit more dagger threes in one game than most teams do in an entire season."*)

After that game, Schertz says, his players became committed to practicing hard and preparing to compete and execute at a high level.

The 'Splitters ripped off eight straight wins, despite two season-ending injuries, and won the SAC regular-season title on the road, defeating Anderson and Wingate. Making it to the tournament championship, they reverted to their old form for one game, getting blown out by Wingate, but in the first round of the regional they beat a great UNC Pembroke team, in what Schertz calls one of the best games he's been part of, by two points. LMU then ran out of steam against a very good Barton College team in the semis. It was the third year in a row that Lincoln Memorial had lost in the second round of the regional tournament.

The Railsplitters were 25-6 on the year; Vincent Bailey (13.5 points per game and 7.4 rebounds) and Jake Troyli (12.6 and 6.1) were named to the SAC's all-conference first team, while Lorenza Ross made the second team.

Lorenza Ross   Jake Troyli

"It's my job as a coach," says Schertz, "to put guys in the best position possible to be successful. You can't always count on the things that have worked before. You have to play to the strengths of your current team.

"You have to evolve, without making any radical changes all at once. Evolution is gradual. I'm constantly studying other teams and coaches, and stealing things we can use. I don't innovate, I borrow. I take things I see and tweak them for our use." (At the time we talked, Schertz had recently made a four-day visit to watch Kansas University practices, with the blessing of Kansas's coach, Bill Self. The sojourn was beneficial: he says that he's come up with a way to tweak his own "fist" offense.)

Over time, the "tweaking" can result in something no longer recognizable as what you had to begin with. As Schertz says:

"What we did six or seven years ago we don't do now."

If Schertz is an inveterate "borrower," he's also a willing giver. In fact, on the day of our interview he is just returned from Richmond, Virginia and the campus of Virginia Commonwealth University, where he was the guest of VCU's newly hired head basketball coach, Will Wade. For fourteen hours or so, Wade had picked Schertz's brain about such matters as offensive schemes, recruiting, and how to rebuild a program and establish a culture of winning.

CHAPTER 9

SCHEMES AND THEMES

The LMU offense, which Coach Will Wade was so eager to pick Josh Schertz's brain about, is a playmaker's offense. It relies on ball screens – meaning that someone comes and sets a screen for the player who has the ball – and provides a good deal of freedom to the playmaker while giving the screeners opportunities to get shots.

The ball screen is beauty and simplicity itself – when it's run correctly. The player setting the screen, after making contact with the playmaker's defender, then "slips" the screen and "rolls" to the basket, or to an open spot where he can receive a pass from the playmaker (the so-called "pick and pop"). The playmaker must come off the screen as tight as he can, shoulder to shoulder, and then must "read" the defense. The defending team has one of three choices: it can double-team the ball handler, leaving the screener-and-roller wide open; it can "hedge" on the screen, meaning that the switching defender comes all the way out to defend the playmaker while the playmaker's defender drops back to guard the roller; or it choose not to jump the ball handler and leaving the ball handler's defender to fend for himself in fighting through the screen, which often allows the playmaker to drive into the lane or all the way to the basket. And it can tear its collective hair out deciding which to do.

The other offensive players, though not directly involved in the play, should be able to either "spot up" or cut and receive a pass from the playmaker if he is allowed to come off the screen and their defenders leave them to help out.

The ball-screen offense can begin with a screen by a big man

SCOTT ERLAND: *"The principles almost always remain the same regardless of opponent. Coach Schertz has a variety of sets at his disposal if there's a particular matchup he wants to exploit, but the basic structure of the offense starts with the ball screen and blossoms out of that."*

The ball screen, from being originally just one option in a team's arsenal of tools, has evolved into an entire offensive philosophy. (It may have trickled down from the NBA, where John Stockton and Karl Malone of the Utah Jazz made it into an art form for the better part of two decades.) It offers multiple opportunities for both screeners and ball handlers. It is free-wheeling, but when deployed by the best offensive teams it has structure and controls built in.

SCOTT E.: *"It (the ball-screen offense) caters to good post players, which we've had lately, and also to playmakers. We've also had good guards, and it gives them a lot of freedom while rewarding creativity. There are countless wrinkles to it, depending on how the opposing team chooses to defend it. The whole idea is to exploit matchups while creating high-quality, efficient shots. The success of it explains why we've consistently ranked among the best in the country in field goal percentage."*

Conversely, when defending against ball screens, Schertz's teams will employ a variety of measures, depending on the players involved in the play. If it's a big guy setting a screen on a guard, the player guarding the big guy will hedge on the screen, forcing the guard away from the basket, while the guard's defender slips "under" the screen and fights back to his man, whereupon the other defender will scramble back to pick up his man, the roller. If it's a guard setting the screen for another guard, the two defenders will simply switch men on the screen.

Coping with ball screens also relies on "help-side" defense, which means that defenders not actively involved in the ball-screen action must be ready to help out in preventing a wide-open shot by the roller or a drive to the basket by the playmaker, while also not losing sight of the player they're guarding.

SCOTT E.: *"It (the LMU defense in general) depends on the size and skill set of the players, but it's all predicated, as everything else is, on ball pressure. And it all comes down to fundamentals. If you can't guard a guy one-on-one, you can't play for Coach Schertz."*

The LMU defense is built on contesting every shot

Defending the post also has its own set of principles. It begins with guarding the post man before the ball even gets to him – that is, by denying him the position he wants to establish for receiving a pass. Schertz's teams will never "front" the post (a maneuver in which the post defender places himself between the post man and the passer), a policy as controversial now as it was shortly after James Naismith nailed up his peach baskets. (Schertz feels that fronting the post puts too much pressure on help-side defenders.) They will try to first force the post player away from his preferred post-up spot; then, if he receives a pass, they will give him an arm's length of space, and when he makes his first move they will immediately "chest up" on him while moving their feet to prevent either a shot or a drive to the basket.

Occasionally, LMU will "blitz" the post, meaning that they will double-team a post man who catches a pass with another big post defender. (They will even more rarely drop a guard down to double-team the post.)

Lincoln Memorial has never run a zone defense in Schertz's tenure there. A zone defense, to his way of thinking, concedes that you can't guard the other team man-to-man. Likewise, his teams will seldom press, as a press, he believes, compromises your man-to-man defense (which is why Schertz wants opponents to press *him*).

SCOTT E.: *"Basically, he wants to take away what the other team wants out of their offense. Giving up an open three-point shot is unforgivable. The rest is dependent on scouting reports and films. In general, we want to make teams uncomfortable."*

Making your opponents uncomfortable sometimes requires making *yourself* uncomfortable. Most players don't regard playing defense as a whole lot of fun. (I didn't, at least.) So, as Coach Pete Carril said:

"The quality that makes the exceptional coach is the ability to get a player to do what he does not want to do, and do it well."

Since Josh Schertz's arrival at Lincoln Memorial, the Railsplitters defensive superiority has been nothing less than astounding. Not ONCE in Schertz's seven years have opponents collectively shot over 40 percent from the field; in the same span, LMU has outscored opponents by an average of almost 14 points a game.

SCOTT E.: *"Defensively, Coach Schertz's teams dominate because of the unbelievable preparation that goes into the game plan. Nobody in the country prepares as thoroughly and as competently as Schertz and his staff do, and Coach Schertz is obsessed with harping on the details in the days, hours and minutes leading up to a game. When a player lacks the attention to detail and the extreme effort that Schertz requires, he doesn't play. Every player is held accountable, and it's produced incredible results."*

The following tells the tale:

Year	LMU FG%	OPP FG%	LMU PPG	OPP PPG
2008-09	.436	.400	72.1	70.5
2009-10	.481	.372	81.9	68.4
2010-11	.495	.392	83.4	66.2
2011-12	.499	.378	79.3	62.3
2012-13	.492	.400	76.5	66.0
2013-14	.502	.394	86.7	71.1
2014-15	.494	.379	80.0	62.8

CHAPTER 10

"I DON'T GET PAID TO COACH"

The 2013-14 campaign, beginning with a host of questions, played out with a resounding answer. Despite the loss of four key seniors from the year before, the Railsplitters reached unprecedented heights with a 28-win season, establishing South Atlantic Conference records for wins (20) and winning percentage (.909). One loss was to Anderson on overtime; another was by two points, at Carson-Newman. The 'Splitters won the SAC regular-season title in handy fashion, and also won the conference tournament.

It was a vintage year for Coach Schertz, and for senior post player Vinnie Bailey. Schertz was named the Red Auerbach College Coach of the Year; Bailey was the conference and region Player of the Year and a consensus first-team All-American.

SCOTT ERLAND: *"Vinnie had the most dominant individual season of anyone during Coach Schertz's* tenure. (He averaged 21.5 points and 10 rebounds in 29 minutes a game, while shooting 62 percent from the field.) It was one of the most enjoyable experiences of my time here, watching him carry the team night in and night out."

Vinnie Bailey dominated in 2013-14

Bailey's fellow senior, Chance Jones, also had a remarkable season, tripling his scoring average from the year before while becoming a lock-down defender, and blooming from role player to All-SAC first team.

LMU, as the two-seed in the regional tournament, beat Carson-Newman in the first round, 76-65. The next day, the Railsplitters played a terrific Montevallo team toe-to-toe for 35 minutes, before running into what Schertz calls "a horrible five-minute stretch at the worst possible time," and losing by a dozen. It was the second loss to Montevallo in the semis in the span of three years, but Schertz concedes that, unlike two years before, Montevallo had the better team.

"This (2013-14) team did the best job of any of our teams of playing to its ceiling on a consistent basis," he says. "It was a difficult way to end a great season, but our guys laid it on the line and maxed out. We just weren't quite good enough to beat Montevallo at their best."

Schertz would face the same questions the next year, after losing his top two players, but he was confident that the system would perpetuate itself – as confident, that is, as someone could be who was congenitally paranoid about things falling apart. ("I always expect the worst," he says.)

It helped that recruiting was becoming a bit easier, given all the success. LMU -- the basketball program, and the university – had a lot to offer.

"It's a great environment," Schertz says. "It's a beautiful campus; it's academically sound, and it's been our mission to develop our players as students as well as athletes. Nineteen out of 20 seniors we've had have graduated, and all four seniors coming up this year are set to graduate." (As a team, the Railsplitters have had the five highest semester GPAs in program history, concurrent with the four winningest seasons.)

"Our basketball facilities – not only the arena itself but the weight room, the locker room, the film room – are as good as any in the country. Our style of play is attractive, and we can honestly tell recruits that we'll be competing for national championships.

"As for player development, we've had players coming out of the program and ending up as pros for five straight seasons." (Following this past (2014-15) season, seniors Lorenza Ross and Keenan Peterson signed on with professional clubs in Switzerland; 2014 graduate Vinnie Bailey, who played -- and dominated -- last year in Germany, is stepping up to the French Pro-B league this season.)

"We've got a good 'product' to sell."

The only fly in the ointment, even Schertz might concede, is the level – or quantity – of fan support.

"We'll probably never pack the place," he says. (Tex Turner Arena seats 5,000.) "That's just because of the way the area is. It's a farming community, and people have work to do at 4 in the afternoon. (Saturday games now start at 4, instead of 8 p.m., as they did until last season.) And on Wednesday, everybody goes to church."

Even so, LMU has led the conference in home attendance for the past several years in a row. And Schertz notes that in 2014, for two of the last three home games of the year, against Carson-Newman and Catawba, a total of 7,100 fans showed up.

He believes that numbers like that are doable for every home game, and he hopes to implement some measures to help attain them, including giving more tickets away and adding halftime entertainment. He'd like to see the top portion of the arena curtained off and all the spectators moved down to the lower bowl, and also the student section positioned next to the opposing bench.

"It's the energy in the building, not necessarily the size of the crowd," he says.

Of course, winning breeds popularity, and there are those who say that LMU basketball will never be a consistent draw until Schertz is able to take his teams further into the NCAA tournament. (Last season's loss to Mt. Olive in the first round of the regional tournament marked the fifth straight season in which LMU has lost in the regional's first or second round.)

"Most people hold others to a much higher standard than they hold themselves," Schertz observes, by way of reply to the criticism. "Some people appreciate your effort and commitment, some don't. And there are some who will never be satisfied."

In his book about a season in the Atlantic Coast Conference, John Feinstein tells of having breakfast in a diner on the morning following North Carolina's upset loss to Arizona in the semifinals of the 1997 Final Four. The Tar Heels had won 28 games that year, with 16-game winning streak. A Carolina fan approached Feinstein and asked him if he thought (North Carolina coach) Dean Smith was "losing it."

Feinstein describes another such incident, when a Wake Forest alum and "fan" collared him to complain about head coach Dave Odom. Wake Forest had missed NCAA tournament five years running before Odom got there; he took them to seven straight tournaments and back-to-back ACC titles in '95 and '96 (Wake had gone 33 years without winning one). The fan was upset that his team hadn't won it again this year. He told Feinstein, referring to Odom, that "We get could a dozen guys to do what he's done."

"Every coach alive is second-guessed by fans, not matter how much he's won or how long he's been a consistent winner," Feinstein concludes.

"I don't get paid for coaching," is how Schertz puts it. "Coaching is the fun part. I get paid for handling the criticism and second-guessing."

And how does he handle it? Philosophically, you could say.

"As you get older, you realize that success and happiness are tied up with the deep and meaningful relationships you have in life. You start to enjoy the journey. The notion – which is a very American one – that you have to win all or nothing, is silly. When I look at the totality of last year, for example, I'm very proud of what we did – how the guys handled things and carried themselves. Besides, we were 30-3; I'll take that every year.

"You can't let others define your success."

Well, you can't always be stoic

CHAPTER 11

A NICE WAY TO LIVE YOUR LIFE

During warmups before every game, the observant LMU fan will notice, Josh Schertz will never make an appearance until just before the game-time buzzer. In fact, Schertz has to be coaxed out of the locker room by his assistants. Dean Smith at North Carolina was the same way; but whereas Smith, a chain-smoker, used the time to savor a last cigarette, Schertz, true to his obsessive nature, will be going over his game plan, like a student cramming for an exam in the hallway outside class.

"I'm a bundle of nerves," Schertz also admits. "The last thing I want to do is be out there. I don't want to see either their guys or ours.

"What if I go out, and see that their guys are never missing a shot? And our guys look cold? It'd just make me more anxious."

So, squirreled away in the dressing room, Schertz will review play sheets, go over all possible situations that might arise and the adjustments that might be deployed, and wrestle with uncertainty. Did we do enough to prepare? Will we execute? Will our effort be there? Have I forgotten anything?

While his players are (he hopes) getting themselves ready, he's getting *himself* ready. And the anxiety will not subside until the ball's thrown up for the opening tap.

"If there's anything that will drive me out of coaching," one ACC coach told Feinstein, "it's waiting for the games to start."

Actually, for Schertz, high anxiety is a year-round, around-the-clock affliction, one that can only be dealt with by ceaseless attention to detail. Such dogged devotion has had its rewards, but it's also come with a cost. Schertz's first wife struggled to understand his job and the hours he chose to put into it, and it contributed, he admits, to their breakup. (Dean Smith's first marriage also crumbled, Feinstein says, even as he started to win.)

Schertz and his wife Natalia have been married for seven years; both their kids, Jordan and Jaden, are from his first marriage. Jaden, who will enter seventh grade this year, plays basketball, and his dad says that while he might be genetically handicapped, the potential is there.

Josh Schertz and his wife, Natalia

Even if Schertz himself had been a giant, you get the feeling he would have chosen coaching over playing.

"You've got a myopic perspective when you're a player, for the most part," he says. "You're all bound up in your own success. It's totally different when you're a coach, or it is to me. You're happy for the success of other people."

He cites Steve Kerr as an example. When the Warriors won the NBA championship, you could see Kerr's pride in his players and his enjoyment of their achievement in his face.

"It's about much more than you," Schertz says. "You feel good for your players, for your assistants, for everyone else involved in the program. It's much more gratifying than any personal satisfaction."

Steve Kerr

Coach Schertz's pride in his players was to reach new heights in 2014-15. Having lost their two leading scorers from the season before, all the Railsplitters did was begin the season 20-0 and climb to number one in the country. For a stretch of time in January, Schertz says, the team played basketball as well as he has ever seen it played.

The streak ended with a loss at home to Carson-Newman, by 15 points. It was a harbinger of things to come. The 'Splitters reeled off nine more wins in a row and easily won the SAC regular-season title (the first team in league history to win three in a row). They weren't playing well, however, and after sneaking into the SAC Tournament finals, they were bludgeoned again by Carson-Newman, mustering only 48 points in another 15-point loss (after having beaten them by 30 at Carson Newman just two weeks before).

In spite of that, LMU secured the number-one seed for the first time in school history, and got to host the Southeast Regional tournament.

Action from the 2014-15 Regional tournament, hosted by LMU

SCOTT ERLAND: "*It was a fun experience for everyone involved, despite how it turned out for our team. We started out by crushing North Greenville (95-62) in the first round, and got ready to face Mount Olive (best known for their pickles). North Greenville had beaten Mount Olive by 2 in their conference tournament finals. Still, it was a bad matchup for us.*

"*We got off to a horrible start. We didn't score for the first six and a half minutes, and didn't make our first field goal until almost ten minutes were gone. We dug ourselves a 22-point hole, and we never could climb out.*"

In spite of its devastating conclusion, 2014 had been a season to top all others under Schertz's sway. The team set new standards for wins (30) and conference wins (21), winning percentage overall (90.9) and in the conference (95.4), and consecutive SAC wins (25).

Still, if you could reasonably say about a 30-3 team that it sometimes lost focus, then you could say that about this team.

SCOTT E.: "*It was weird. We only had three losses, but they were all blowouts. At the end of the season we'd lost confidence in our shooting. We were pressing. Mount*

Olive had a good game plan. They roughed us up; they forced us to do some things we didn't want to do. That's how Carson-Newman beat us twice – they were tough and physical. I think the loss to Carson Newman at home, after we'd won 20 in a row and were number one, was horribly deflating."

The 2014-15 Railsplitters had an historic season

"It's a very volatile business," Schertz says of his chosen field, coaching college basketball. "You're putting your life in the hands of 18- to 21-year-olds." Which is to say that, sometimes, no matter how hard you try or how well you prepare, you can't control everything."

Nevertheless, Schertz is doing what he loves, and how many of us can say that?

"I always wanted to work with kids," he says. "I wanted to impact their lives. In coaching, you get to do that every day. From doing drills to scrimmaging to sitting and watching tapes, you can see them taking things in and growing and developing as people.

"Most of our guys have been high-character, easy to coach. We've had some great players, and we've had some guys who didn't get a lot of minutes but were always ready to go. Guys like Hunter Spaw (a six-foot junior guard from Bean Station, TN), who practices as hard as he can without much reward, and keeps up his attitude and is always a good teammate."

SCOTT E.: *"Coach Schertz has always kept the proper perspective. He's always seen that a college career is to prepare you for life, because basketball eventually will end."*

Schertz points out with pride that some of his ex-players are coaches, while some are still playing ball, and others are in the corporate world. Five of them have Masters degrees. Most of them, he's still in touch with.

"I'm glad I've been able to be part of their lives to one degree or another."

Dean Smith, who coached for 36 years at North Carolina, said that as he grew older, the one constant in his life was his contact with ex-players. He said that it was that aspect of his father's career as a coach – how his former players would make a point of coming back to see him – that may have inspired him to be a coach as well. Said Smith:

"It just seemed like a nice way to live your life."

CHAPTER 12

ONWARD AND UPWARD

In his seven seasons at LMU, Josh Schertz has won 170 games, or an average of 24 games a year. Excluding his first, get-acclimated season, he has averaged 26 wins per year. Should Schertz be able to maintain that lofty average while coaching another 27 years, until he's 67 (the age at which Dean Smith retired), he'll have 872 wins, only seven short of Smith's career total of 879. Is that realistic?

"A coach's life is precarious," wrote Pete Carril in his book, *The Smart Take from the Strong*. But Schertz's doesn't seem to be, particularly. He enters this season with a lifetime contract to coach at Lincoln Memorial. Considering the talent he's been able to lure to Harrogate, and the job he's done marshalling that talent, it appears that nothing, barring illness or death, will slow Schertz's ascent to the rarefied air of 800-plus victories.

SCOTT ERLAND: *"There's a seismic shift going on with the team. Last season, for the first time ever, our top three scorers were guards. In the six previous seasons that Coach Schertz was here, a guard never led the team in scoring, and only once were one of our top two scorers not forwards. This coming season, our best scorers will be guards. It will be interesting to see how he adapts to this situation, but it's certain that he will."*

"I'm intrinsically motivated," says Schertz. "I want to continue to improve as a coach and a leader, and to always get kids who will represent the university, who will graduate and be successful when they leave.

"I recognize how lucky I am. This was a real bad job when I got here. Since then, the level of commitment to the program has been second to none. It's crazy to think that so much has happened. Now, you can argue that this is the best Division II job in the country.

"I want to reward their faith in me."

"The boy's beguilement with a sport never wholly evaporates." – Phillip Roth.

I came to Harrogate to look into an obsession, and after I did it was no less a mystery to me. Why Josh Schertz is as crazy about coaching basketball as I was about playing it is as unexplainable as any passion.

"For those of us who coach," was all Schertz could tell me, "it's in our blood. We have to do it."

Likewise, I had to write something about Coach Schertz, even if it wouldn't solve anything. I found the process therapeutic if not curative – I suppose I'll always be "a little bit off" about basketball. I mean therapeutic in the sense of being bracing, as it always is when you probe another mind and find a kindred spirit. And for once, the writing wasn't an ordeal.

I'll give my son Scott the last word:

"It's easy to write about Coach Schertz and LMU basketball. They write themselves."

The Railsplitters under Josh Schertz, season by season

By Scott Erland

Trophy basketballs from Josh Shertz's seven seasons at LMU

2008-09

Coach Schertz's first season can only be described as a rollercoaster, but even that was considered a tremendous improvement following an eight-win season in 2007-08. The Railsplitters went 14-14, with a number of impressive wins and some at least mildly embarrassing losses. With a team comprised almost entirely of freshmen, and other players with little to no college experience, the Railsplitters were a scrappy bunch, challenging the best in the South Atlantic Conference at times. They made the first statement win of the Schertz era on January 21, 2009, defeating the 11th-ranked Catawba Indians by 15 at Tex Turner Arena. The Railsplitters finished 8-8 in SAC play after going just 1-13 the year before, and earned a spot in the conference tournament. It was a mediocre season by some teams' standards, but for those familiar with the LMU men's basketball program, it was a significant cultural shift.

2009-10

The Railsplitters made another leap forward in Schertz's second season, winning 20 games for the first time in the school's NCAA Division II era. LMU won 14 of its first 16 games before faltering a bit down the stretch, finishing the season with a 20-9 record. Despite the second-half skid, the Railsplitters earned the opportunity to host their quarterfinal round match-up in the SAC tournament, where they outlasted Mars Hill 83-70, and advanced to the semifinals to face Catawba. The Railsplitters nearly pulled off another stunner, leading by as many as 10 points in the first half, but fell a bit short in a 70-60 loss. If not for some shocking upsets around the Southeast Region, the Railsplitters would have earned a bid to the NCAA tournament that season, but it wasn't yet to be.

2010-11

This was the season when everything officially changed, and the Railsplitters became the alpha dogs of the South Atlantic Conference. Lincoln Memorial opened the season by winning its first 22 games, breaking the program and conference record for longest winning streak. On December 8, having dominated their first seven games, the Railsplitters broke into the top top-25 national rankings for the first time in program history. Despite dropping back-to-back nail biters in February, the Railsplitters went on to win their first-ever SAC regular season and tournament championships, while also earning the program's first bid to the NCAA tournament. Lincoln Memorial suffered a shocking loss in the opening round of the Southeast Regional, but still completed the season with a 27-3 record, tying the conference's single-season record for wins. Schertz was recognized as the SAC Coach of the Year, while Desmond Johnson was named Player of the Year.

2011-12

The Railsplitters made history again in 2011-12. After starting the season with a perfect 14-0 record, Lincoln Memorial moved to No. 1 in the NABC national poll for the first time in program history. The Railsplitters celebrated that achievement by destroying Mars Hill 131-96 at Tex Turner Arena to win their 15th straight. After that dazzling start, the Railsplitters hit a bit of a lull, losing four of their last 13 regular-season games to finish second in the SAC race. LMU was upset in the semifinals of the league tournament, but still earned a return trip to the NCAA tournament. There, the Railsplitters were able to do what they couldn't the season before: win a game. LMU defeated King 67-60 on March 10 to win the first NCAA tournament game in program history. In the second round of the regional, the Railsplitters were eliminated by Montevallo in arguably the most heartbreaking loss in program history. LMU led that game by 14 points with eight minutes to go, but the Falcons clawed all the way back and stole a 61-60 win on a last-second bucket. Montevallo went on to play in the national championship game that season.

2012-13

The Railsplitters didn't have a winning streak exceeding eight games during the 2012-13 season, but they were able to put together a 25-6 overall record and capture the program's second South Atlantic Conference regular season championship. Two highlights of the season were the Railsplitters pounding 12th-ranked Augusta State by 14 points on the road, and having a game broadcast to a national television audience via the CBS Sports Network. Lincoln Memorial lost in the championship game of the SAC tournament before advancing to the second round of the NCAA tournament with a thrilling 82-80 win over UNC Pembroke, pulled out by Lorenza Ross's last-second heroics. Hot-shooting Barton ended the Railsplitters' season in the semifinals of the Southeast Regional.

2013-14

This was the season of Vincent Bailey, who was named first-team All-American after averaging 21.5 points and 10 rebounds per game. Bailey and Chance Jones (15.1 points/game) led the Railsplitters to a 28-3 record (the league single-season record for wins and winning percentage), SAC regular season and tournament championships, and into the second round of the NCAA tournament. Schertz was voted the SAC Coach of the Year for the second time, won the Red Auerbach Coach of the Year award, and was named a finalist for the Clarence Gaines Award. The Railsplitters led for nearly 35 minutes of their Southeast Regional semifinal game against Montevallo, but the Falcons turned it on late and handed Lincoln Memorial a 98-86 loss. The Railsplitters completed the season ranked No. 6 in the national poll, the program's highest-ever final ranking.

2014-15

The 2014-15 season was one of the most accomplished in the history of the program and the South Atlantic Conference, as the Railsplitters went 30-3, matching the 1976-77 team for the most wins in school history and breaking the SAC record for wins and winning percentage. They opened the season with 20 consecutive wins, eventually moving to No. One in the national rankings for the second time in program history. LMU went on to win its third straight SAC regular season title while also earning the opportunity to host the NCAA Southeast Regional. The Railsplitters destroyed North Greenville 95-62 in front of a raucous Tex Turner Arena crowd, to advance to the second round of the NCAA tournament for the fourth straight year. Unfortunately, they were unable to make it any further, as Mount Olive upset the top-ranked Railsplitters to end the season. Lorenza Ross was the SAC Player of the Year, while Schertz earned his third SAC Coach of the Year honor.

Get there early next season and if you're lucky you could get your own Josh Schertz bobblehead

ABOUT THE AUTHORS

Paul Erland is a writer living in Nashville. Email him at *paulerland@gmail.com*.

Scott Erland is Lincoln Memorial University's Director of Athletic Communications. Email him at *scott.erland@lmu.net*.

ACKNOWLEDGMENTS

The authors would like to thank Josh Schertz for his kindness, patience and generosity in the making of this book.

Made in the USA
Lexington, KY
10 November 2018